Loon Legends

Loon Legends

*A collection of tales based
on legends as retold by*
Corinne A. Dwyer

Illustrated by
Mark Coyle

NORTH STAR PRESS of St. Cloud
St. Cloud, Minnesota

Dedication

To
John & Rita
Cecelia, Miranda & Elizabeth

A special thanks to the Central Minnesota Writers'
Workshop for their encouragement and critiques.

Artistic contributors: Mary Jo Pauly & Cindy Pintok

Cover art: *Morning Reflections*, painting by Derk Hansen

Second Printing: May 1989

Library of Congress Catalog Card Number: 88-060995
International Standard Book Number: 0-87839-046-4

Published by:
North Star Press of St. Cloud, Inc.
P.O. Box 451
St. Cloud, Minnesota 56302

Contents

Loon Legends

Mark Coyle

Introduction

he loon glided into the bay as the sun climbed down the branches of the crooked pines. He rode deep, only his black head and white-banded neck arched above the skin of water. The tiny swirls and tremors he made in the evening-stilled bay dissipated almost as soon as he passed, yet the disturbance was enough that the chorus of frogs paused in their incessant chirps, beeps and gulps as he swam along the shore just beyond the reed beds.

Insects—gnats and black flies by the tens of millions—swarmed in soft, undulating clouds through the stiff, thin reed stems. Tiny fingerling perch kissed at the surface making little pops and concentric ripples as they fed on the gnats which touched the tension skin and adhered to the water. As the loon passed, they too paused in their eager feeding and darted away. The loon swam on.

Away from the wide, clear-watered main lake which reflected the evening sky's mellowing hues, shadows swallowed the remains of the day and, like the swarming gnats, thickened about the loon's head. The loon swam on.

1

Mist began to rise and cluster against the shore. The loon became a solitary ghost sliding through malevolent, black waters. The stillness of the evening larger than the whining of insects and the moaning of frogs began to weigh heavily on the bay, silencing the drone and depressing the hunger of the fingerlings. Stillness, like the mist, muffled the shore and pressed outward over the water. The loon swam on.

The bay bellied out where the shoreline turned back on itself toward the main lake. Reed-thin spruce ringed the final pocket of water. The naked spines of long-dead trees stood before the clotted blackness of the spruce in several feet of oozy, death-smelling, muddy swamp. Cattails and reeds clumped between the stagnant water and the clean, cold water of the bay where the loon finally paused in his steady course. In the center of this small arena, facing out toward the main lake and the fading turquoise of the western sky, the loon waited. Silence closed in around him. The first stars winked on as the evening sky deepened. The loon, resting still in the glass-smooth water, listened for an endless moment. Listened. Waited.

Then, like Lancelot drawing the jeweled Excalibre from cold, black waters, the loon lifted his sharp bill in song. Clear yet haunting notes rose above the stillness, challenging it, subduing it. Again and again the loon sent his laughing tremolo and long wail up into the perfect night air. And like echoes with independent voices, other loons took up the song. From all over the main lake, the loon's call was augmented and then repeated to other loons too distant to hear the first notes. Other lakes began to answer, repeating the melody for still more distant loons to hear. For many minutes the lone loon sang and was answered in ancient Gavian symphony. Then, as suddenly as it had begun, the song was over and the loon fell silent. More slowly, the many other voices quieted until a complete stillness settled over the lake country.

Then, the spell wavered. An owl hooted in five soft even notes. There was a stirring in the dry grasses near the shore as mice and voles began to scuttle about. The yellow eyes of a lynx briefly caught the reflected light of the moon. With a sudden, sharp cry, a rabbit met the talons of a hunting owl. This was followed by an almost grieving silence—one long moment—the length of time the night paused for the death of a rabbit. Then, as the last paleness tarnished in the west and the black sky blazed with gnat-like millions, the sounds and odors and movements of night began their course.

The fire reached up from the tangle of logs. The flames, like imagination, were more colorful, more graceful than the charred disorder of fallen wood. And like imagination, the flames were fueled by the sober reality of life and death— fueled by it, not limited by it. The fire created its own reality. It created its own wind and rose on it. Like a bright, translucent being, it danced a dance of its own making, charged by the heat of its own being. It challenged the cloak of night with its brightness and threw sparks to ignite the stars.

Faces surrounded the fire. Caught in the ruddy light, they were changed, distorted. The fire played a magic on each one in different ways. A child, asleep in his mother's arms, lost the soft roundness of youth and became aged. The mother, slightly in profile, had shadows playing over her face which suggested an owl under her skin. The old man with the drum was a red-masked shaman counting out an ancient rhythm of spells and magic. The rest—the two boys nodding sleepily together, the men back from the lake, the woman finished with the tasks of the day—they had become altered, strange. They waited for the storyteller to begin.

The drum beat slowly, catching the rhythm of the fire,

matching the rhythm of the night. The old man listened to the night and the lake and the forest. He heard the loon and the owl, the lynx and the rabbit. He was preparing himself, drawing up the stories from deep within him. That is where the best stories come from—the soul. And since each soul is different, touched by life uniquely, each story, though re-peated time after time, is different, cast by the soul of the teller, caught by the magic of the fire and drawn away by the smoke, up, up into the night.

Mark Coyle

Mark Coyle

The Loon's Necklace

I will begin the story telling," said the old man. He held the drum lovingly in his hands and turned it so he held a certain side in his left hand.

"This drum has been at story-fires for more years than I can remember," he said. "My father and grandfather used it when they told stories around their camp-fires. Maybe this drum was used by people so long ago that the stories told to its beat were new stories. Legends we now re-peat with reverence were once just little stories people told to explain the things they saw or events which occurred. Maybe some were told to ease the tired children to sleep."

The old man smiled at the mother with the child in her arms. The child had stirred at the sound of the drum and whimpered briefly. The mother put the baby to her breast and returned the old man's smile. The baby settled into its meal and slumber.

A loon sang out on the lake. Another answered from the distance. The people listened until the duet was over.

"So many voices tonight," said the old man. "I think per-haps the loons are prompting me. The legend I wish to recount

7

this evening is the Loon's Necklace."

The woman with the child hummed approval, and others around the fire nodded or smiled.

"Good," said the old man. "Then I will begin. 'An old man who was recently blind lived with his wife and young son near a great lake like this one—'"

"Wait," said the mother. "You have told this story before and it has always bothered me that it begins this way—in the middle. Certainly it's possible for an old man to have a wife young enough to have a 'young son,' but to say he was 'recently blind' leads me to feel the story is not begun at the right place. How did the old man come by a young wife and become blind?"

The old man regarded her with amusement. "That is another tale."

"One you have never told," returned the woman.

"Then I will tell the entire story tonight," smiled the old man, "though I wonder if your interest is the story or the continued beat of the drum that might keep your son asleep."

Several laughed, including the mother.

"Tell the story, but . . . if it would not intrude on your tale, use that quiet, soothing voice of yours and a soft beat to the drum."

The old man chuckled and nodded. He closed his eyes for a few moments as he beat the drum with a regular rhythm.

"Yes," he said, "it fits the tale of the Loon's Necklace."

There was a young man who was a great hunter. His name was He-who-hunts. His arrows always flew to their mark. Even in lean winters, when the wolves howled in hunger, his family ate well. He knew where the deer fed; he could find the rabbit deep in its thicket; and when he fished, his basket always came home full.

When the time came for him to wish a wife, many young women sought his favor. Only two interested him, a shy young woman with long hair and soft eyes, and a bold woman who enticed him with flashing eyes and a teasing smile. But because He-who-hunts was a quiet man used to the still forest and whispering pines, he found Speaks-softly, the shy woman, more to his liking. They were married and set up a lodge of their own.

The bold woman was very angry that He-who-hunts did not choose her. She went in search of the Owl-woman, her mother. But, before she reached the secret lodge deep in the forest where the Owl-woman lived, a large bear attacked the young woman and killed her.

Owl-woman found her daughter's body and grieved her loss for one whole year. Then she swore she would avenge the death of her child and went to the village to learn how her daughter happened to be in the forest alone.

The people were very much afraid of Owl-woman, for she was wicked and could call magic against them. When Owl-woman demanded to know why her daughter was alone in the forest, the villagers told her the story of how He-who-hunts had chosen another over her daughter.

"How can that be?" said Owl-woman. "My daughter was lovely to look upon. She was young and beautiful. She worked very hard. What else would a hunter want in a wife?"

The mother of the woman He-who-hunts married spoke up. "Your daughter was indeed very beautiful, Owl-woman. She was easily the most beautiful woman in the village. But He-who-hunts is such a shy man. Your daughter was simply too bold for him. He is a quiet man, with quiet ways. He chose a wife like himself, quiet and shy."

"Quiet and shy. Quiet and shy," Owl-woman mocked. "His life *was* quiet. Because of him my daughter is dead—"

"It was a bear that killed your child," said the mother of the shy woman. "He-who-hunts knew nothing of this. He is not responsible."

"He is if I hold him so," shrieked Owl-woman. "Bring me this man and his wife. Bring them to me at once or all the village will be punished."

"He is not here," said the brother of He-who-hunts. "He has not been in the village for several months. This spring, even before the ice left the lakes, He-who-hunts and his wife took their newborn son away from here."

"I do not believe you," screamed Owl-woman and she began to search through the village. The people were too afraid of her to stop her. Even still, Owl-woman destroyed everything in her path. Pots and baskets were broken, stored food scattered in the dirt, and even the lodges were torn and burned. When there was no place left in the village where even a small child might hide, Owl-woman left and began to search for He-who-hunts.

He-who-hunts and his wife, Speaks-softly, had indeed left the village some time before. Speaks-softly had given birth to a son late in the winter and the baby was very tiny, sickly and weak. When he almost died in a fever, the young couple had decided to travel to the Great Lake and beseech Loon to help their son. Just as the magical bird had arrived

at the lake, tired and hungry from his long migration, He-who-hunts went out in his canoe and offered Loon food. The great bird was grateful. He-who-hunts then offered to defend Loon's nest all that season if he would grant a request. Loon listened, then agreed. By the time He-who-hunts had paddled back to the lodge he had made for his wife, the baby was no longer ill and began to thrive.

He-who-hunts was very happy. He stayed in this lodge and hunted in the forest to feed his family. Part of each kill he shared with Loon.

One night a horrible screeching woke the couple and made the baby cry. He-who-hunts took up his bow and knife and went out to see what was causing the fearful sound. He saw nothing and the shrieking stopped. He returned to the lodge just as Speaks-softly blew the smoldering coals into flames. When He-who-hunts entered the lodge, she took up a fire-brand and held it before her, afraid.

"What is it?" He-who-hunts said fearfully and spun to look behind him. No one was there. He secured the entrance and turned back to his wife. She had dropped the branch and was staring at him, her hands over her mouth, her eyes wide and dark with fear.

"What is it?" He-who-hunts repeated, a knot of panic beginning to burn deep within him.

"You," Speaks-softly stammered. "You ... your face! What happened to your face?"

"I don't understand," said He-who-hunts, dropping his bow and reached up with both hands to touch his face. The texture was foreign, like worn leather, like the aged cheek of his mother before she died. He splashed water into a bowl and took up the fire-brand Speaks-softly had dropped. Held high, the ruddy torch revealed his reflection in the water. To

He-who-hunts' horror, the face of an old man stared back at him from the bowl.

He-who-hunts dropped the clay vessel. It struck one of the rocks surrounding the hearth and broke neatly in two. The water soaked into the dirt floor on the one side and hissed into the coals of the hearth on the other. Outside a cackling began. It was the laughter of an old woman. He-who-hunts flung open the door and saw an old hag cavorting in the clearing in front of his lodge. He-who-hunts knew who the old woman was.

"Why have you done this to me, Owl-woman?" he asked, extending his weathered, knobby hands to her imploringly. "What have I done to you that you have made me into an old man?"

Owl-woman abruptly stopped her crazy dance and approached him slowly, her step the stalk of a cat on the hunt. Her eyes glared a glowing red in the night. "You did not choose my daughter as your wife," she told him. "You broke her heart. She died in the forest coming to me with her grief."

"No," said He-who-hunts, "she did not love me. She was angry when I chose Speaks-softly and threatened to have you cast an evil spell on me. She was going to you in revenge, not in sorrow. I would have thought you would have seen this in her and refused her request. I thought you were wiser—"

"My daughter is dead!" shouted the old hag. She rushed at He-who-hunts, her hands like claws reaching for his face. He-who-hunts had his knife ready, but before she reached him, she changed into an owl and flew at his head. He slashed at the bird, but was so startled at the transformation that he missed. A moment later, high in the top of a black spruce, the insane shrieking of a screech owl began, ending in the crazed laughter of Owl-woman.

12

He-who-hunts returned to his wife. "Pack everything we can carry," he told her. "It is Owl-woman who did this to me. I fear she will not let us live even after turning me into an old man. When the day is strong and she is asleep in the black spruce, we must flee this place and hide from her."

The next day, He-who-hunts led his wife deep into the forest along trails so hidden that even rabbits and deer did not know of them. By evening when Owl-woman woke, they were far away and hidden. Her shrieking did not bring anyone out of the lodge and the baby did not awaken and cry. Owl-woman changed back into an old woman and entered the shelter. When she discovered that He-who-hunts and his wife had fled, she was very angry and began to search for them.

He-who-hunts was a great hunter and was as stealthy as the animals he hunted. For eight years he was able to hide his family from Owl-woman's searching eyes. But he was also now an old man. His back ached when he got up in the mornings; his knees hurt by the end of the day. The endless moving and watchful hiding wore at him constantly. Finally, he knew he could no longer travel if he was going to be able to provide for his family and growing son. He built a lodge in a deep glen and rested.

As it had happened eight years earlier, He-who-hunts and Speaks-softly were awakened one night by harsh shrieks. Their son Loon's-gift woke also and crawled over to his parents. He-who-hunts was just struggling to his feet.

"Don't go out," Speaks-softly pleaded. "It's the Owl-woman. I just know it is. If you go out into the night, I am afraid she will hurt you."

He-who-hunts groaned his way up from his mat and sighed, "What more can she do to me. I am an old man nearing the end of his life. If I go out, maybe I can keep her from harm-

ing you and Loon's-gift."

He-who-hunts took his bow and his knife and went out into the clearing in front of the lodge. It was a black, moonless night, and clouded over so that even the brightness of the stars was excluded from the darkness. He-who-hunts could see nothing. The screams stopped anyway so he groped his way back to the lodge door and slipped inside.

"Light the fire," he whispered to his wife. "Light the fire so I may secure the doorway."

Speaks-softly did not respond right away. He-who-hunts turned to her, his arms hanging limp at his sides. "The fire is lit, isn't it?" he said softly.

"Yes," was her faint response.

In a moment she was sobbing, her arms wrapped around He-who-hunts' neck. "Why did she do this to you?" she asked. "How could even she be so cruel as to make you an old man ... and then make you blind?"

*   *   *   *   *

It was very difficult for the family in the next several weeks. Owl-woman shrieked from the top of the red pines every night and sometimes dove at them during the day. Once she tangled her talons in Speaks-softly's hair, pulling out clumps of it when she flew off. Their stores of food dwindled. He-who-hunts could no longer see to aim his arrows. They ate what roots Speaks-softly grubbed up and small birds Loon's-gift took with his sling. Spring rains came, and for five days there was no going out, nor small game about if Loon's-gift did try to hunt.

"We are out of food," Speaks-softly said sadly.

He-who-hunts hung his head. For a long time he said

14

nothing. But then his chin lifted and his shoulders firmed with determination.

"We must go to Loon," he said. "Loon has the power to help us. Loon's magic is greater than Owl-woman's. Tomorrow we must sneak away and go to the Great Lake and find Loon."

Owl-woman shrieked all that night to try to ruin their sleep, but He-who-hunts slept anyway, sure an end would come soon to the threat from the old hag.

In the morning, when the racket had ceased and He-who-hunts felt Owl-woman was asleep, he and his family slipped into the forest. Escape was very difficult this time because he could not see, but Speaks-softly and Loon's-gift had learned much forest lore in the years of hiding. They were able to keep ahead of Owl-woman's relentless pursuit.

It was a four-day trek to Great Lake, made more difficult by the lack of food. On the evening of the fourth day, when the scent of water on the wind blowing off the Great Lake was in their nostrils, He-who-hunts told Speaks-softly and Loon's-gift to make a shelter before nightfall. Speaks-softly went in search of a cave or thorny thicket while He-who-hunts sat by a stream to rest. Loon's-gift sat at his side and watched the tops of the trees for Owl-woman. He-who-hunts was just drifting into slumber when he felt Loon's-gift stiffen at his side.

"What is it?" He-who-hunts whispered, afraid it might be Owl-woman.

"A bear," said Loon's-gift. "There's a bear just across the stream. It's very near."

An idea came to He-who-hunts. "I will draw my bow, son. Aim the point of my arrow at the bear's heart and tell me when to let fly the shaft."

The old man notched his arrow to the bow string and

the boy guided his aim.

"Now, father! Now!" Loon's-gift called out.

He-who-hunts released the feathered shaft. He heard it *thunk* into the bear's body. By the very sound of it, he knew it had reached the bear's heart. There was a splash as the huge bear collapsed, its head resting in the stream's flow.

Loon's-gift was jumping up and down with joy. He-who-hunts smiled and patted his son's shoulder. "Between us— a blind old man and a boy without the strength to draw the shaft—we still make a good hunter! Quickly, son, take my knife and cut us meat for our supper. Tomorrow you and your mother can dry the rest of it. Hurry, though, night must be falling soon; I can hear the insects singing their evening chorus. If Owl-woman is near, she will beset us soon."

Owl-woman was near. Very near. She watched from the swaying top of a white pine as the boy waded through the stream and began to cut a haunch of meat from the bear. She waited while he skinned the flank and began to slice great ribbons of meat from the thigh. Then she shrieked her dreadful scream and chortled when the boy leaped up from his work and splashed his panicked way back across the stream.

Owl-woman did not follow him, nor make much note of where He-who-hunts and his son went. Instead, she flew down to the fallen bear and gulped down the long strips of flesh the boy had cut up. As she fed, she cackled and made her plans.

*   *   *   *   *

The family huddled in the mouth of a damp cave. They spoke very little, but their bellies complained about the lost meat. Finally, He-who-hunts crawled to the back of the cave

16

and lay down.

"It's going to get very cold in the next days," he told his wife. "I can feel a spring storm in my bones. If we are going to ask Loon's help, we must do it tomorrow. But if Owl-woman knows I'm going to solicit Loon's magic against hers, she's sure to try to stop me. As weak as we are now, she might just succeed. If she keeps me from Loon, we will die."

Speaks-softly spoke. "Then tomorrow Loon's-gift and I will go to the bear."

"Owl-woman will be there and could hurt you, even if her magic is weaker during the day."

But Speaks-softly put her hand on his cheek. "But if she is bothering us, then you might be able to make it to the Great Lake and Loon. Do you think you can find the lake on your own?"

"Yes," smiled He-who-hunts. "Yes! We are so close to the lake that I could find it by the sound of the wind on the water and the smell of the breezes that course its waves. And if the two of you are at the bear, Owl-woman will think I am too weak and helpless to be off on my own. It's a dangerous plan but a good one . . . perhaps the only one that will work."

"But what will you give Loon? We gave him all that we had when Loon's-gift was a baby. What is left?"

The smile that had begun at the wrinkled corners of He-who-hunts' mouth slipped away. "We have no food to offer. All the riches we had were given to make our son strong. It's true, there is nothing to give."

Speaks-softly reached into her amulet pouch and took out a necklace of tiny polished shells. "It's not much," she sighed, "and it is so old that I no longer wear it for fear the frayed lacing that holds them will break and scatter the shells into the dust, but it is a pretty thing . . . "

17

"No, you must not give that. It was your great-grand-mother's necklace. I will think of another—"

"No," Speaks-softly said firmly. "No! You must take it. What is a shell necklace compared to our lives?"

She opened his gnarled hand and folded his fingers over the smooth shells.

The next morning, after Speaks-softly and Loon's-gift left with food baskets to try to get some of the bear meat, He-who-hunts slipped from the cave and made his way in the direction of the lake. It took him longer than he had hoped—he fell often on protruding roots and had to try several times to make his way around deadfalls—but when he finally stood on the shore of the Great Lake, a peace filled him. He listened to the waves lap the shore. The breezes brushed softly against his cheeks. And from far out over the water, the magical cry of Loon came to his ears.

He-who-hunts called to Loon. Loon answered. The old man called again. This time when Loon answered, the note was from much nearer. He-who-hunts called one more time, and Loon answered from near at hand.

"Who is it who calls to me?" Loon asked.

"It is I, He-who-hunts."

"You have aged most markedly in the last few years."

"This is the work of Owl-woman. But I am not so concerned with being old as I am with being blind. I cannot provide for my wife and young son, the son you filled with your strength. In any case, the small gift I have to offer you is not enough to pay you for assisting me with both afflictions. If I could just see . . . "

"What is it you offer?" Loon said.

He-who-hunts took the shell necklace from his pocket and held it up for Loon to see. "It is but a small gift, I know," said He-who-hunts, "and there is nothing more."

"Then for the sake of the child that carries my strength, I will accept the necklace and help you to see. But even if I restore your sight, how are you going to protect yourself from Owl-woman's anger? She could make you blind again . . . or worse. Your request seems futile to me."

The old man sighed. "What else can I do?"

After a pause, Loon said. "Come into the water with me. Take hold of my wings as I dive."

He-who-hunts waded into the cold water and took firm hold of the great bird's wings at the shoulders. Loon dove. As cold closed over He-who-hunts' head, he feared he would never see the light of day again. Loon was a powerful creature whose magic was very strong, but Loon did not always give as one might wish. The fear in He-who-hunts' heart did not last but a moment, then He-who-hunts pushed it from his mind.

They seemed to be going down forever, but then Loon stopped the powerful thrusts of his feet and He-who-hunts could feel them rise. They broke the surface just as he was sure his lungs would burst.

"Can you see?" asked Loon.

He-who-hunts gulped in air and wiped the water from his eyes before he spoke. "No," he moaned. "No, I can see nothing!"

"Then you must dive with me again. This time do not fear me."

Again they went down, and as the water closed over him for the second time, He-who-hunts wondered if Loon could really restore his sight. As before, this feeling lasted just a moment and was gone.

This dive seemed longer than the first. He-who-hunts felt himself grow dizzy before they burst into the air. He gasped for breath over and over, unable to fill his lungs enough.

"Can you see now?" asked Loon.

He-who-hunts strained and squinted about himself. "I can see the sun sparkle on the water and some shadows at the shore, but nothing more. I cannot see enough to hunt."

"Then we must dive again. This time do not doubt me. Bury your face in the feathers of my back and think of nothing."

Ashamed, He-who-hunts took hold of Loon's wings again and was pulled into the cold water of the lake. This time he blanked his mind before any thoughts took hold of him and buried his face in the black feathers of Loon's back.

The dive was endless. He-who-hunts was out of air before Loon had stopped stroking with his powerful feet. He knew he could not make it to the surface. In another moment, he lost consciousness completely, his mind filled only with the swirling blackness of the water and the press of cold around him.

He-who-hunts awoke to find himself lying in the pebbly shallows with gentle waves lapping at his feet. He sat up and pressed his palms to his eyes because they hurt with a white pain. But even as he did this, He-who-hunts realized that what he felt was the brilliance of sunlight after so many days of total darkness. Slowly he opened his eyes and rejoiced in the blueness of the sky and the blue-green of the water. He could see!

Loon waited just off shore. He-who-hunts had no words to express the gratitude that welled up in his throat. Instead of trying to mouth inadequate words, he took the necklace from his pocket and flung it toward Loon. Even mid-air, the string that held the shells loosened and released the hundreds of tiny polished shells. Loon spread his wings. The shells

20

fell against the velvet black of his plumage. A magic turned the shells to feathers; the string coiled into barred markings at Loon's throat and neck. Then the great bird bowed to the old man and turned to swim out onto the vast lake.

*　*　*　*　*

He-who-hunts hurried back to the cave and slipped in. A little while later, his wife and son stumbled in. Speaks-softly was bleeding from her scalp and several long scratches on her face. Loon's-gift was holding his arm where owl talons had closed on him. But they had a basket full of bear meat to show for their injuries.

He-who-hunts gave them a sign to remain quiet, and whispered the wonderful news that he could see. They carefully blocked the entrance to the cave and roasted great strips of meat. They feasted as they had not in a long, long time.

As his aged bones had told him, the weather lost the softness of spring during the night. The wind rose until it screamed louder than Owl-woman's wailing, and the temperature steadily fell. By morning, snow turned the forest an impenetrable white.

Inside the cave it was warm. The bear meat filled them and would last several days. The family settled into their furs and were content to wait out the storm.

That night, above the harsh wind and the moaning of the pines, Owl-woman could be heard. Her shrieks, however, were edged with fear. All night she screamed, but in the voice of an old woman, not a bird. Just before dawn, she fell silent at last.

Behind the pile of stones and dirt with which He-who-hunts had blocked the cave entrance to keep out the wind and snow, the family slept into the morning, at peace at last without Owl-woman's disturbances.

When He-who-hunts stretched and finally rose from his mat, he was pleased to discover he was not as achy as had become usual. "The storm is passing," he told Speaks-softly.

She did not answer him, and when he met her eyes, He-who-hunts saw that they were filled with astonishment. And she was staring at him. He-who-hunts looked at his hands and felt his face. The wrinkles and creases were no longer there. He felt his youthful strength when he flexed his arms. He was young again! He knew then that Owl-woman had died in the night. He was free from her vengeful wrath forever.

Just then, Loon called from the lake, his song easily cutting through the lessened wind.

"Loon did this for us," He-who-hunts said. "As an owl, Owl-woman could have survived the blizzard . . . but not as the old woman she really was. I think Loon made another magic besides restoring my sight. To keep our son alive—the child filled with his strength—Loon changed Owl-woman from bird to person and she died in the storm. For all our days we must remember the debt we owe Loon."

The next day, while spring warmed back into the lake country, the family began their journey back to their village.

The old man set down the drum. A loon called out on the lake. He smiled, wrinkles filling up his cheeks.

"I have never doubted the magic of the loon," he said softly. "You can hear it in his voice. I just wish I had the courage to follow Loon down into the black waters of the lake. Or even the nerve to ask him for my youth. And then I have to wonder . . . would he take another necklace? I don't know, but I'm ready if he would." And he took from his pocket a string of tiny, polished shells and tossed them lightly in his hand.

Mark Coyle

Loon-woman

Across the fire from the old man sat the woman with the young child in her lap. The baby had settled into sleep as the old man told his story and remained asleep after he was finished. The woman nodded at the old man and smiled. In a voice carefully modulated to reach his ears yet not wake her child, she said, "I have a story I could tell."

The old man with the drum stopped the slow rhythm of his palm and met her eyes. He smiled. For a moment, he held out the drum as if to the fire, then passed it to the man next to him, to begin its journey around the fire. The young man, a strikingly handsome fellow, passed the drum to the woman next to him. She fairly snatched it from his fingers and held it to her breast a moment before reaching past her sister who sat next to her.

The woman with the child was the next person in the circle. She looked at the drum held stiffly toward her. Instead of immediately taking it, however, she slowly eased her sleeping child to a blanket at her side and covered him carefully. Only then did she take the drum.

The mother's eyes slipped from the triumphant face of the woman who had given her the drum to the downcast head of the sister, then to the eyes of the handsome man. A knowledge passed from her eyes to his. He averted his gaze, embarrassed. The mother sighed and began to beat the drum.

She tapped the taut skin of the drum head with long fingers. The tempo of her beat was different from the slow, steady rhythm the old man had maintained. Hers was quicker and at the same time quieter.

The fire filled the woman's face with shadows and the patterns of other-worldly places. It experimented with tints of color—burnt orange, deep mauve, rich russet—trying to capture the creatures within her. But the woman's face constantly shifted, eluding definition, as if she contained a power greater than the fire's own.

The people around the fire waited. The old man, his story told, settled into himself, seemingly nearing the euphoria of sleep. The others were more expectant. They watched the fire dance to the drum and the smoke slide to the stars. The boys counted the beings under the woman's skin.

A loon of the lake fell in love with a beautiful woman and made a magic to become a man so that he could be with her. When he did not return to the loon community, his relatives imagined he had been killed by the people.

"No," said his sister. "I believe he has found the love he wanted. If the woman had rejected him, he would have come straight back to us. Only a fool would think him dead."

"Only a fool would assume instant success," an old loon returned.

"Nonsense!" said the sister. "Why, even I could find love among humans if I wanted too. In fact, I *do* want to. It would certainly be a more pleasant life than living among such ridiculous simpletons!"

And so, loon created a magic which made her into a woman. But it was not a good magic. Though she saw herself as a lovely young woman with graceful lines and a sweet disposition, in reality—in the eyes of the people of the village—she was an ugly creature, half loon, half woman. She had short legs, a thick, curveless body and a long pointed nose. In spite of her distorted appearance, she might still have found a companion, except that the sweet temperament she imagined she possessed was a vindictive, argumentative, shrewish humor which no one wanted. This was the real reason she had failed to find a mate even among the loons of the lake.

Loon-woman discovered that the villagers did not want her among them, and she was too ashamed to take back her form so soon after the boasting she had done to the loons on the lake about how easily she would attract a human male. Instead of going back to the loons, she wandered deep into the forest.

27

For many years she remained alone, becoming even more sour of humor and more distorted of form. Her hair, instead of being soft and flowing, was a tangle of feather-barbs that no preening would soften or make shine. Her eyes became red, glowing coals and her feet were clawed and webbed. People fled from her in terror and no loon would answer her croaking call. She had become an evil witch-creature shunned by all.

Then one day in early spring, Loon-woman was wandering along a stream, trying not to hear the music of the water, nor see its playful splash over stones. It looked too much like joy. She considered damming the stream and filling it with mud. Where the stream widened into a pool and a grassy bank had grown thick and soft, Loon-woman paused. She knelt down on the spongy bank and tried to stare into the dark depths of the pool, seeking a magic of black waters.

Before she had whispered the chant to call the blackness to her, she spied something clinging to a reed at the edge of the pool. She reached for it. As her fingers touched it, it clung to her hand. She examined it. By holding one end and slipping it through the wet fingers of her other hand, she extended it. It was a hair, but not her hair, not her coarse, dull feather-barbed hair. As the strand dried in the sun, stretched between her hands, it was soft and supple and fine.

Loon-woman studied the hair, pulling it slowly across her palm, rolling it between thumb and fingers. She tried to envision where it had come from, whose hair it had been. A thought came to her and she closed the hair in her fist, thrusting it deep into her pocket.

"Anything so fine," she muttered to herself (for she always muttered to herself), "will surely be missed. If I had hair so fine and soft, I would count each strand. If one should

fall, I would gather it up and braid it into a necklace strung with beads."

So, expecting the owner to come back in search of the hair, Loon-woman hid herself and waited. The sun scaled the mountain of sky and began its tumble to twilight. No one came past the pool. Loon-woman kept to her thicket, ignoring the rumble in her belly and the thirst in her throat even though the pool was but a few strides away.

Night came. The stars wheeled like swallows. Loon-woman could hear the stream, the wind and the small creatures of the night, but no person came in search of the hair. By morning, she could no longer keep to her hiding place and crawled to the pool to drink. She lay flat on her broad belly and leaned over the grasses to sip at the cool water. She paused, then sipped again. When she paused the second time, she saw a reflection in the pool behind the dark, swirling image of her own face.

She rolled to her back and was almost shocked to find that she was still alone. Her loneliness so flooded over her then that she scrambled to her feet and ran into the woods, her arms thrown up over her eyes that streamed hot tears. She ran until her breath gave out and the battering of branches and brambles had cut and beaten her almost senseless. Then, falling to the ground, she cried until her eyes were emptied.

In the next several days as Loon-woman wandered the forest aimlessly, she began to dream of the person from whom the hair had fallen. It was a man, in her mind's eye—tall, strong and handsome beyond words. And, of course, this wonderful man loved her alone and cared for her alone as no man had ever cared for woman. This was her fantasy, and it began to dominate and fill her mind.

She took the strand of hair and strung on it many tiny

white shells as small as the nail of a baby's smallest finger. With the ends tied together, the hair was long enough to make a bracelet. It was her most treasured possession.

One day late in the summer, when the days had dried to leather and heat shimmered against the morning sun, Loon-woman again found herself near the pool with the grassy bank. The water was no longer sweet with melted snow, but had become like the season, thick and sour—almost fermented with heat. Still, in a time of great dryness, when stream after stream flowed only with rounded stones, any water was welcome. Loon-woman leaned over the brown tangle of grasses at the bank and reached down a cupped palm to bring the tepid water to her lips. Three times she did this, easing her thirst. As the last drips of water slid from her fingers, something still clung to her hand. She looked at it. It was a hair, a soft strand the twin of the one she wore strung with shells on her wrist.

With trembling hands she drew its length between her fingers and watched the sun dry it to a glossy sheen. For many hours she sat by the pool caressing the hair as she envisioned the man who had owned it might caress her. Then she took a pouch from her pocket. It was just a circle of leather gathered at the edge with a thin leather lace. She dumped the contents of the pouch into her lap. Hundreds of tiny shells, each no larger than the nail of a baby's smallest finger, scattered over the leather of her shirt.

Loon-woman strung the white shells onto the hair, and taking apart her bracelet, added the new strand to make a necklace. It was well after dark before she finished and slipped the necklace over her head. But she had forgotten that there was a magic in stringing beads by the light of the moon. There was a Magic of Apartness in making circles in the dark. Loon-

woman thought only of the man of her dreams and did not remember the magic of the night. Had she, she might have stopped. But she made the necklace of hairs and the hundred white shells no larger than the nail of a baby's smallest finger and put it on as the stars filled the sky around the moon. Then she crawled into the thicket near the pool and slept.

In the morning, from the thicket where she lay, Loon-woman heard voices. Voices! She had not heard the voices of human beings in many years, except the screams and shouts to make her go away from those she chanced to meet. She crawled nearer the pool so she could see who spoke.

A woman leaned over the bank at the pool, filling a slick skin with water. She was slender and smooth and young. Standing near her, holding two dripping skin flasks was a man. Loon-woman stared at him, her heart beating so quickly, she felt faint. His hair shone in the morning sun. It was smooth and soft and tied at his neck with beaded leather. He was tall, strong and very handsome. This was the man whose hair circles her neck. This was the man of her dreams.

Loon-woman stood and walked from the thicket. The man saw her first, and stared at her, his expression forming question, then disgust. His companion sat back on her heels, saw Loon-woman and screamed. As she scrambled to her feet, the man stepped forward a step.

"Who are you?" he asked softly.

"I am your lover," Loon-woman breathed and walked toward him on her short legs, her arms open to embrace him.

But the man drew his hunting knife from the sheath on his thigh and held it before him. He drew the young woman behind him and slowly moved back.

"You are Loon-woman," he said, then. "I have seen signs that you were around here. Please go. We wish you no harm,

but you are not wanted here."

Loon-woman stopped and dropped her hands to her sides. "But you are my lover," she said sadly.

"Not me," the man said quickly, his face tight with disgust. "Not me, old woman."

In a moment the handsome man and the young woman were gone. Loon-woman was alone by the pool. For a long time she just stood where she had stopped and stared into the forest where the two had gone. But though she made no sound nor moved from the spot, within her heart she was nurturing an anger. Her lover had rejected her. The young woman had stolen her man. The delicate fantasy of gentle love had become twisted by the Magic of Apartness she had brought on herself by stringing beads in the light of the moon, by making circles in the dark. Hatred overcame love in the twisting of magic of the night.

All around her the forest quieted, stilled by the intensity of the emotion that she felt. The birds did not sing, the red squirrels did not chatter, and the deer moved out of that section of woods even though drawn by the water. The water itself, darkened and muddied; the trees around her wilted.

Loon-woman made a plan to seek out this man and tell his people that he had abused her love. She would demand that he be returned to her or she would bring harm on them all. And when he was returned to her, she would make him her servant and treat him as he had treated her. Thus filled with purpose, Loon-woman found the trail the two had taken and followed them.

But the man had been clever. A short distance into the forest, he had hidden their tracks. Loon-woman wandered the woods well into night, her anger growing at each waddling step. She found their camp early the next morning. It was

deep in the forest, in a glen surrounded by steep ridges clothed in pines. It was the smoke of their cooking fire rising straight up on the still morning air that she saw from the ridge and followed.

The young woman stood at an open fire roasting fish. She saw Loon-woman and stared a moment, then ran to a shelter and ducked in. In a moment, the handsome man who had accompanied the young woman to the pool and another, younger man came out to stand between the shelter and Loon-woman. An old man struggled after them on short, thick legs. He made his way next to the man Loon-woman wanted.

"What is it you want here?" the old man croaked at Loon-woman.

She pointed at the tall, handsome man. "That man is my lover. But the girl has turned him from me. I want him back and I want her punished."

The handsome man tensed and was about to speak, but the old man touched his arm and stepped forward. "This is my son. He is not your lover. The girl is his wife. The other man is my younger son. He is not your lover either. Perhaps you are mistaken and it is another man who spurned you."

"Do you think me a fool that I cannot recognize my lover?" Loon-woman said. "He is my lover all right and I want him back. Give him to me."

"No, Loon-woman. Perhaps we can offer you food or a warm blanket instead."

"I don't want your food," she spat, "and I don't want your thin blankets!"

With that, she rushed forward to grab the handsome man's arm. He pushed at her and she fell in the dirt. She tried to rise and the younger brother shoved her with his foot. Her

face hit the dirt, filling her mouth with dust. She lifted her head and spat it out.

"No! No!" the old man was shouting to his sons. "Let her be."

He took her arm to help her rise, but Loon-woman hit at his hand and struggled to her feet unassisted. She wiped her mouth and face on her sleeve.

"My sons are young," the old man said apologetically. "They do not respect age as they should. Forgive them the brashness of youth."

"Father," said the younger son, "why do you treat her like kin? She is a witch and a beggar. Here . . . here is a stick. Let's beat her off so she will not return."

"Hush!" said the old man angrily. "Loon-woman is not a beggar. Let her go her way unharmed."

When the old man looked back at Loon-woman, there was a sadness in the depths of his eyes. Loon-woman gathered herself and slowly withdrew from them. She vanished into the forest.

The old man turned to his sons. "Now we must leave this place. She is angry and can do us great harm."

"She is a foolish old hag," grumbled the younger son.

But the older one had seen his father's sadness. He did not understand it, but he did respect it. "Father is right," he said softly. "We must leave."

"Yes," agreed the old man. "She is more powerful than you can imagine. In her eyes I could see something terrifying. I do not wish to stay and discover too late how dangerous she is. Gather all you can carry. We must leave right away."

But before they had broken camp, the older son shouted, "Look! On the ridge!"

His brother and father and young wife looked where he

pointed. Smoke filled the eastern sky, blocking the sun.

"And look!" cried the woman, pointing to the west. More smoke tarnished the sky. "We must hurry."

"Wait!" said the old man. "We are too late, I fear. There is no fleeing now." And he sat down next to the smoldering cooking fire.

The younger son pulled roughly at his shirt. "Father! Are you mad? We will be burned to death if we stay here. We must run for our lives."

The old man was putting wood to the hot coals. He shook his head. "There is no means of escape by normal routes now. Now we must rely on magic. You asked me why I treated Loon-woman like kin. She is kin. Loon-woman is my sister, though I doubt she recognized me. But our mother came to me when my sister became human. It was a long, long time ago. She gave me an amulet against Loon-woman. Come my sons and wife of my son. Sit with me while I make a magic to protect us against Loon-woman's."

Reluctantly, the men and woman sat at the fire as the old man asked. They silently watched as he took from his neck a worn leather bag. It was no more than a circle of leather gathered with sinew. The old man opened the leather until it lay flat on the ground in front of him. On it there were dozens of white shells no larger than the fingernail of a baby's smallest finger, some sinew thread, and a small leather pouch. This last the old man took up and blew into it. It filled with air, forming a small round sack held shut by the old man's fingers.

"What is that?" the younger son asked.

"It is the crop of a loon. It is powerful magic. I think it is the right one to save us. I do not know that for certain, though. It has been many years since my mother gave these

things to me and told me of their use. If I remember her in-
structions, this little bubble can carry us up over the fire and
safely away from this place. The one caution mother gave
me with its use is that once we begin to use it, we must not
look back until the magic is over. I am not sure what will happen if we disobey, but I suggest we do as we are told."

"But how can a little bubble blown in a loon's crop save
us from the fire?" asked the sceptical younger son.

"We shall see," was all his father said. The old man held
the dried crop over the fire. The hot smoke filled it and it
swelled. Soon it was twice the size of the tiny bubble the old
man had held in his hand.

"Get a wooden bowl," he told the woman. He gave the
swelling crop to the older son to hold over the smoke while
he bored four holes in the rim of the bowl. With the sinew
thread he tied the bowl to the loon crop.

"This is foolishness," said the younger son. "We are wast-
ing precious time. The fire—"

"Do not look at the fire now," warned the old man. Then
he cocked an eyebrow at the young man. "If you knew how
much you remind me of my sister, you would believe in what
I have told you. But the magic is working. Watch it and trust
in it."

Soon the crop was bigger than the fire and growing larger
by the moment. The bowl was also getting bigger, as if it could
take in the hot air from the fire. The threads fastening the
bowl to the crop were thickening also.

"Fetch a rope!" shouted the old man. "We must hold
down the sky basket until it can carry us all."

The older son did as bidden and pounded stakes into
the ground around the fire to restrain the swelling crop balloon, now the size of the shelter.

When the bowl had grown big enough to hold them all, the old man ordered them into it. The leather crop was huge now and straining at the ropes that tethered it to the ground. In a moment it would pull free and take the people to safety in the sky.

Smoke from the forest fire was making them all cough and choke now. The heat caused their skin to glisten with sweat. The old man made them sit in the bottom of the bowl so they could not peek out.

One rope pulled free of the stake and the sky basket lurched, pulling at an angle at the other two ropes.

The blood-red of fire and black of smoke filled the sky above them. Flames burst into the trees around the camp. Fearful, the woman screamed and her husband held her closely against his breast.

The sky basket broke free of its second trace and heaved over on its side, caught between the pull of the leather balloon and the tautness of the last rope.

"Shall I cut the rope, father?" the younger son shouted over the roar of the raging fire.

"Yes! Cut it . . . but do not look at the fire or Loon-woman if she is near!"

The man could easily steel himself against looking at the fire. He had seen fire raging before and had no need to look upon it again. But as he hacked at the rope so tense it was as hard as stone, he could not keep himself from peeking into the clearing of their camp. Through the flames that burned everywhere except right where the sky basket stood, Loon-woman danced a wild victory dance, a dance of revenge fulfilled.

At the moment he looked, the sky basket shuddered and began to deflate. The old man gasped in horror. He knew

they would be burned to death if the balloon collapsed. He thrust his hand into his pouch again strung on his neck. With a fistful of white shells in his hand, he looked to see the direction of his son's gaze. Then, holding his other hand tightly over his eyes, he stood and threw the shells at Loon-woman.

In that instant, his son fell back into the bowl of the sky basket and the huge balloon billowed full again. The rope snapped apart, weakened from blows of the knife.

With a rush, the sky basket rose up into the sky. In but a moment it was above the heat and smoke and calmly floated away from the fire. The sky basket landed far away from the Loon-woman's forest. The old man and his family never returned to that part of the lake country again.

It is said that Loon-woman died in the fire she had made and her soul became again a loon. The necklace of tiny shells no larger than the fingernail of a baby's smallest finger became the neck markings and the pattern of white spots across the loon's back. The fire is said to have purged Loon-woman's soul of the evil she had possessed, so that when she became a bird again, she was finally able to find the mate she had sought for so many years.

On the night air heavy with summer heat, the clear warble of a loon's tremolo climbed. There was a crispness to the call that spoke of deep, clear water—water that never lost the north's cold. Though shallow bays and the surface of the lake warmed during long summer days, the loon hunted down in the dayless winter waters where the fish flashed like stars. Its wail carried the lonesomeness of windswept ice and its tremolo the knowledge that, in the northland, summer was a shimmering film of warmth that spread over the land, not a welling up of heat from within. The magic of the north was that cold always underlaid warmth. The loon knew this secret. The loon revelled in magic.

The handsome man—twenty-five and fairly tall—smiled warmly at the woman with the baby as he listened to the loon calling out on the lake. The woman took her child back into her arms and then met his gaze. Her smile was small, almost hidden, but he saw it and returned a wide grin. The woman took up the drum and tossed it to him. He caught it easily and passed it back to the old man.

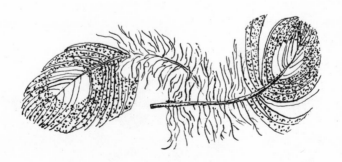

Mark Coyle

Creation

wo boys were among the people at the fire.
The older one, a twelve-year-old, reached
toward the old man with hands that were
widening with manhood.

"Grandfather," he said, "could I tell
a story?"

The old man smiled teasingly. "You could, if you have
a story to tell. Which one are you considering?"

The boy was serious. "The old, old one . . . the creation
story."

The old man was pleased. "A very fine choice! It has been
many story-fires since I've heard that one. Are you sure,
though, that you remember it well enough to tell it?"

"I've heard you tell it many, many times, Grandfather.
I'm sure I remember it exactly right."

The old man smiled and held out the drum. The boy
grinned proudly as he took it, but as he settled it in his lap,
he hesitated before touching the taut skin top. Suddenly he
was shy.

The other boy, his ten-year-old brother, elbowed him hard
in the ribs.

"Give me the drum then," the younger brother said loudly as he tried to snatch it away. "Give it to me. I can tell that story better than you anyway. And I'm *not* scared!"

The older boy held onto the drum and moved it out of his brother's reach. He frowned and shoved the smaller boy's shoulder away from him. But he had taken courage from the teasing and hit the top of the drum with the flat of his palm. The drum boomed. He cringed and looked first at the frown of the woman with the child, then at his grandfather.

The old man smiled gently and mimed a softer touch. The boy tried it and the drum purred out its rhythm. He gave his little brother a haughty look and then turned his attention to the fire.

At the end of the woman's tale the adults had settled into their own quiet conversation. When the drum beat began again, even if it was slightly irregular and varied a bit in rhythm, they ceased their own talk and gave the boy their attention. The boy felt this and felt almost like the adult he would soon grow to be.

At first there was just sky. It was big and grey and filled with brown swirls which were like clouds but were not clouds. This was the place of the Creator. He liked it there. But after a while, he grew tired of this place and longed for some company. He searched for another place to find companionship, but could not. There were no other living beings except himself. It was then Creator decided to make creatures for his world.

Creator experimented with many kinds of living beings, all shaped from the swirling browns and greys. Some he gave soft grey fur and legs; others he fashioned with wings and feathers. He made small animals like the tiny shrew and great huge ones like the bear. Very soon, Creator learned that he liked making creatures and began to have more fun with them. He took up a mouse and stretched its forelegs into wings and set it on the wind. He blew on the long fur of another until it dried and stiffened into rattling quills. And one big deer he gave long, awkward legs and flattened its huge antlers. But he made the nose of this one too big. He was about to change it, but then didn't.

All the birds and fish and mammals were colored in shades of brown and grey. These were the colors of Creator's world, and were the only colors he knew.

Creator worked a long time on these creatures until he ran out of ideas and variations. The space about him was filled with them and they floated about quite peacefully as if in a misty cloud. But after admiring his work for some time, Creator discovered that he was still lonely. He still had no one to keep him company. The only solution was to make a creature somewhat like himself. Creator did this.

The human he had created was a boy. As he floated about

Creator's head, the boy said, "What is this place where you have me bobbing about? What must I do here?"

Creator was thrilled the boy could talk to him. "You don't have to *do* anything! Just keep me company and talk to me."

"If I am to talk with you," said the boy, "perhaps I could come and sit on your knee. It is very hard to concentrate while I'm bumping about among all these animals."

Creator took the boy from the misty cloud and sat him on his knee. Together they discussed the rest of the living things Creator had made. They laughed about the moose and the porcupine and the bat. In fact, the boy was a wonder at naming things and called the owl "Great Horned" and the hard-shelled reptile "Turtle."

"I wonder," said the boy, "could I try my hand at designing an animal?"

"Oh, yes!" said Creator. "That sounds like great fun! What would you like to make?"

"A bird, I think. Yes, a biggish bird. It should have . . . a long, sharp bill . . . smooth sides . . . and strong wings."

As the boy told him his plan for the bird, Creator molded it in his hands. "What else? I have merganzers and ducks not much different than your bird."

The boy thought carefully. "I think it should be a different color from your birds, something else besides all the browns and greys."

Creator was intrigued. "What do you mean? There are no other colors."

"In my mind I can see others," said the boy. "Darken the grey to its deepest shadow . . . until it is so dark, you can no longer see grey."

Creator did this, covering the bird entirely in black feathers.

The boy looked at the result critically. "That's too dark ... no, not too dark, maybe, but too much. Put spots all over its back and wings and lighten its breast through the palest greys until there is no color again."

Now the bird was black with row upon row of white spots on its back and a white breast. Creator was so fascinated by this process of lightening and darkening the grey tones, he experimented with markings on the neck that alternated black and white bands.

"That's very nice!" agreed the boy, "but don't use up all that nice dark color. Let's make a new color."

Eagerly Creator agreed. He took up a lump of the black color and rolled it between his palms. Harder and harder he pressed as he rolled until the heat building within the ball made it glow an intense, brilliant red.

"Look at this!" said Creator. "Look what I have made! Do you want some of this fine ... 'red' on your bird?"

The boy examined the red color and said, "Just a little bit, maybe. Make the eyes red."

Creator was a little disappointed. He made the boy's bird's eyes red, but began to dab the red on other creatures as well. One of the crow's relatives he shaded black and painted its shoulder with red. He splashed red on the sides of some fish and spattered it on other birds that flew passed him.

But soon the red lump was used up. Creator looked at the boy, who was sitting with the bird he had designed in his lap, stroking the glossy white-speckled black feathers.

"Help me make other colors," said Creator. "I like colors."

"What would happen," answered the boy, "if you rolled another black lump until it turns red ... but kept on rolling it?"

That was an interesting idea. Creator did it. As the lump

glowed vivid red, he continued to roll it faster and faster in his palms. Soon the red shone like a flame—a bright, hot yellow.

"Do you want some of this color on your bird?" asked Creator.

The boy studied his bird. "I've grown fond of him just as he is. Use your new color on other creatures."

Creator was disappointed only for a moment. Then he was sprinkling yellow about. Some fell in the wolf's and lynx's eyes and dripped on the head of one blackbird. Many fish swam through swirls of it, and one little warbler fell right into the color and had to be fished out.

On his own, Creator thought to mix the red and yellow. Soon he was painting bright orange about. He was having immense fun.

"Leave some brown and grey animals," said the boy. "Those are nice colors for fur. It makes them look warmer."

When Creator finished with his lump of orange, he looked again at the boy. His smile fell. The boy was just sitting there on his knee stroking the big bird.

"Have you named your bird?" asked Creator softly.

"Yes," said the boy. "This is Loon."

"Does Loon make you sad?"

"Oh, no," the boy said, looking up. "It's just that I don't think any of the animals, except the birds, maybe, are really happy bobbing about in the mist. I've been thinking that there ought to be a place for them so that the animals can walk about and stretch their legs and the fish can swish their tails and swim and the birds can land and rest."

This made a kind of sense to Creator. He thought a long time about how this could be achieved. Then, he reached up with widely spread hands and pushed down the swirling mist

of browns and greys until an empty space was made and the colors swirled and flowed only below his knees.

Except for the birds which fluttered even harder to stay in the air, all the creatures fell from the sky into this sea of swirling browns and greys.

"What have you done?" exclaimed the boy.

"I've made a place for the creatures to rest apon."

The boy looked about him. "The fish seem quite content and some of the birds can sit upon the water, but look at the rest. They are splashing about and gasping for air. I don't think this is the right place for all of them. And the birds flying about look as if they are getting tired and want to rest."

The loon in the boy's lap began to struggle to get into the water. Afraid for his friend, the boy tried to hold the loon back. In the end, both tumbled off Creator's knee and splashed into the water. Loon was happy there and swam and dove through the waves; but the boy coughed and choked and thrashed about like many of the other beasts. Finally, he bumped into the shell of a huge turtle and crawled up onto the bony plates of its back.

"How do you like water?" asked Creator.

The boy choked a bit more, then said, "Interesting, but I am not as content in it as a fish. Make a place for creatures who do not like water as well as fish and ducks."

"Oh, I will, I will . . . but not right now. Now I want to make a new color."

The boy sat at the edge of the turtle's shell and fished out as many of the smaller creatures as he could so they could rest and dry off. But even though it was a really huge turtle, soon all the space was taken. The moose and deer, the bear and wolf were too large for him to lift out, and even if he could have managed it, there was no room for them on the crowded

back of the turtle.

"What we need," said the boy as he watched their struggle, "is either a bigger turtle shell or something else solid and dry."

Creator did not hear him. "What other color do you have in your mind?" he asked the boy.

"Forget about colors," said the boy. "These creatures need help. They cannot swim much longer."

Creator frowned. "You are not helping me. Where are all the fish? I can't see them."

"The fish are in the water. You can't see them because of the browns and greys."

"Then I'll clear the water!" said Creator.

In a moment he had pushed the swirling colors deep below the surface of the water, making it so clear that each fish could be seen swimming in schools and shoals.

"If the world were brighter," said the boy, "we could see the fish's colors better."

"Yes!" said Creator, and he fashioned a huge fiery yellow ball and set it high in the sky. The light made the fish flash with color and the warmth dried the wet creatures on the turtle's shell. Even the water of the great sea began to warm and sparkle in the light.

"Now for my new color!" said Creator. "Now I want you to help me with the new color!"

"But the creatures," began the boy, but he stopped when he saw Creator getting angry. The boy sat back on his heels and sighed. "It is your world. I suppose we should do it your way. Why don't you see what happens when you take up a handful of water and compress it in your hands."

Creator eagerly scooped up some water and tried to squeeze it. It rained down on the sea. He tried again. Again it

ran out of his hands and sprinkled over the sea.

"Try drying it out," suggested the boy.

Creator cupped his huge hands and held his palms to the sun. The heat steamed away the water in great billows and clouds. Nothing was left. Creator did this several times more hoping it would begin to work. No new color formed. But the great white clouds grew thicker and soon were storming over the sea and soaking the boy and animals on the turtle's back. But when the clouds thinned and the sun shone through the last mist, a rainbow was formed.

"Look at the colors!" exclaimed Creator. "Here are *all* the colors!"

While the rainbow lasted, Creator studied the colors in it and picked out his favorite—blue. He washed the whole sky in it, using so much that it dripped into the water and colored it blue also. Then Creator got up and began to dance over the water in his joy at finding all the colors.

"Now help the animals," said the boy. "You said you would make a place for them."

The boy could see that Creator no longer was paying any attention to him, no longer knew he existed. As Creator danced away, admiring his blue sky and sea, the boy realized it was up to him to save the animals before they drowned.

Looking through the crystal sea, past the many schools of fish, the boy could see the browns and greys that Creator had pushed below the water. He wondered if some of those thickened colors could be added to the edge of the turtle's shell to make a place for the animals. He dove into the sea, intending to swim down and bring some up, but he was not far under the surface when he knew he could not possibly swim down far enough to reach the layer of muddy colors. The boy scrambled back onto the turtle's shell and wondered

what to do.

A muskrat swam past his foot that trailed in the sea. It had rested on the shell, but seemed equally comfortable in the water.

"Muskrat," said the boy, "dive down to the mud below the sea and bring some back for me so I can make a place for others to rest."

The muskrat dove. The boy watched as the little beast stroked with webbed feet and receded into the depths. As he watched, the muskrat turned and started back up well before reaching the bottom of the sea. Soon the swimming became frantic, then quite suddenly stopped. The body of the little muskrat floated to the surface and the boy scooped it up into his hands and cried.

The loon swam to the edge of the shell at the boy's feet. He saw how sad the boy was and knew what he had to do. The loon dove. The boy tried to call him back, but his words did not go beneath the waves. He could only watch as his friend receded into the depths of the sea.

With great strokes of his feet, the loon swam much faster than the muskrat had. The boy was fearful and hopeful at the same time. And then, when the loon was very small, the boy saw the layer of color move. The loon had touched it, scooped up a billful and began to swim to the surface. It took a long time, but with each powerful push of his webbed feet, the bird got bigger, closer to the surface. Sadly, just feet before the loon reached the air, he stopped swimming and floated slowly up. The boy reached into the sea and lifted the lifeless body of the loon from the waves. In its mouth was some mud from the bottom of the sea.

Even as the boy cried at the loss of his special friend, he tried to stick the mud to the edge of the turtle's shell to make

enough room for the rest of the animals to climb on and rest. But the little bit the loon had carried up was not enough to make anything. The boy had lost the muskrat and the loon and still had no way to help the other animals.

Just then, Creator returned. "I'm sorry," he said. "I forgot about you."

"Look," cried the boy. "Muskrat is dead. Loon is dead. They tried to get me some mud so I could make a dry place for them."

Creator reached down and brought up great waves of mud which quickly dried in the warm sun.

"Not everywhere," cautioned the boy. "Some creatures like the water."

"I know," smiled Creator. "Look! I have made dry places and still have seas left. I even made some little puddles on the land and put fish in them. And I splashed green all about. I like green too. Do you like this place I've made?"

The turtle crawled up onto the land. The moose and bear, the deer and the wolf swam to the shore and rested in the sand of the beach. The birds flew down chirping to the branches of trees. The boy walked on the brown and grey of the land.

"Yes," he said, "yes, this is a wonderful place."

Creator held his closed fist down to boy and slowly opened it. Sitting quite comfortably in his palm were the loon and the muskrat, restored to life.

"Yes," the boy said again. "This is a place where I will live."

"Good," said Creator, "because when I was wandering just now, I found another place I would like to explore. I will be back another time when I am finished my travels."

The boy stopped beating the drum and looked to his grandfather. The old man rubbed his chin and smiled.

"That was not exactly the version of the creation story I seem to remember telling you," he said.

The boy grinned. "No, it was better! I didn't like it that the muskrat reached the mud and the loon didn't. I wanted the loon to be the hero."

"I see," said the old man, raising an eyebrow.

And the boy drew quite serious and said, "That is the way the story goes in my heart, Grandfather. You always told me to tell a story the way it was in my soul."

And the old man nodded as he reached for the drum.

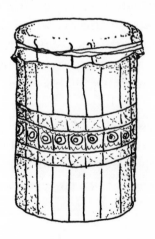

Mary Jo Pauly

Mark Coyle

The Loon, the Owl and the Snipe

The younger brother snatched the drum from the older boy's hands.

"My turn!" he announced.

The older brother tried to take back the drum and admonished, "You have to ask Grandfather for it. You can't just take the drum."

"Can to! I can tell a story, can't I, Grandfather?"

The woman with the sleeping infant said, "Wake the baby and you'll get no turn. Give the drum to Grandfather and ask for it respectfully or I might just say it is getting too late for any more storytelling."

When the younger boy hesitated, the older brother elbowed his ribs. The little boy pushed back, then handed the drum back to the old man and said, "I would like to tell a story now. Could I tell one, Grandfather?"

The old man accepted the drum and smiled with the patience of ages. "The storytelling is open to anyone to relate a tale and for all to enjoy. What legend do you remember that you would like us to hear?"

"The one after the creation . . . when all the birds picked a leader . . . you know, the one about the loon, the owl and

55

the snipe. I remember it better than *he* remembered the creation story." And he looked down his nose at his brother, which was difficult as his brother was taller. But little brothers all know how to do it—tilt back the head and stare down the nose with half-closed eyes.

The older boy smirked and elbowed him just hard enough to get even, not hard enough to get in trouble for hurting his pesky sibling. The littler boy dared to poke him back, an act he knew could not produce retaliation without adult intervention.

The old man, who missed nothing of this exchange, gave his grandson a warning glance as he handed him the drum. When the boy attempted to take it from his hands, the old man resisted, causing the lad to meet his eyes in question. Softly, the grandfather whispered, "The story-fire is not a place for battles."

The little boy knew better than to be too sassy with his grandfather and looked down. "Yes, Grandfather. Can I tell my story now?"

The old man released the drum into his young hands. The boy grinned with pride and settled himself with the drum between his knees. He raised his hand quite high to strike the drum, but the woman with the baby clucked her tongue and he looked at her. She pursed her lips and shook her head in tiny little jerks.

The boy deflated just a little and sighed. When he began to play the drum, the beat was neither too fast nor too loud. The woman nodded her approval and smiled. The boy settled into the rhythm, stared into the fire and readied himself to tell the tale.

After all the world was made and all the animals had found homes in it, groups began to pick leaders for their kind. The fish that swam the cold northern lakes chose the pike as the leader of the fishes. All the fish respected the northern pike for his speed and sleekness and teeth, especially his teeth.

The land animals had to choose from the bear, the wolf and the moose. Leadership went to the wolf because the bear slept all winter long and the moose was hunted by the wolf.

The birds were having a hard time picking a leader.

"I vote for Great Horned Owl," said Jay. "There's no bird more fearful, more powerful, or more watchful than Owl."

"But Owl doesn't even swim!" complained Black Duck. "How can the leader of the birds be someone who doesn't know how to swim?"

"What about Canada Goose?" suggested Crow.

"No, no, please," said Goose. "Forgive me, but I don't *want* to be leader. I have far too many children to raise to worry about the rest of you. Let someone be leader who has less to do."

Owl strode to the middle of the gathering, his long, black talons clicking on the stone shelf at the shore of the lake where they had gathered together. "There, see!" he boomed. "Goose does not want to be leader. Let it fall to me." And he fluffed out his feathers until he was huge, shook himself and settled his feathers again. He slowly twisted his great head all the way from one side to the other so that each bird had the full benefit of his yellow-eyed stare. Then he closed his eyes to slits and settled deep in his down to wait for eveyone to agree.

Chickadee, Jay and Raven all clapped their wings together, quite satisfied with Owl as their leader. Jay was already trying

to think how a profit could be made on it.

Black Duck, who made sure he was quite far from Owl's wicked talons, said, "There is another problem. Owl does not go south for the winter. The leader of the birds should lead the way south when it is time to go and pick the time to come north again in the spring."

Jay, who stayed in the frozen north, saw no profit in a leader who went south. He told them this. Then, one of the warbler cousins spoke up. "What about Snipe? Snipe is a shorebird so he knows both water and forest and he goes south each fall and comes back north in the spring."

Owl hooted his outrage and Crow cackled in scorn. Jay said, "We will not be led by little Snipe! Not little shy Snipe. There's no profit in that. Pick another!"

Loon had been listening to all the fighting. He did not want to be leader of all the birds, but Snipe was his friend and he did not like to see him treated badly. He said, "Let me be leader, then. I am not a little, shy bird. I sing loud enough to be heard by all and brave the night with my calling. I am a waterbird and can fly strongly also. *And* I go south for the winter."

Snipe tugged at his wing and whispered, "But you don't know directions well enough to lead a migration."

"Hush!" whispered Loon. "Owl doesn't know that."

Owl was stomping up and down, his talons drumming on the stone. "What are we who stay north in the winter to do when all you good folks leave each fall? I don't like it that the leader is going away at a time of year that is hard and needs good leadership. Satisfy that!"

They argued a long, long time. Finally, it was decided that Loon would be the leader of the birds, but stay north very late into the fall and return very early in spring. During

the winter the northern birds would look to Owl as leader until Loon came back in the spring. Everyone seemed satisfied. Satisfied, that is, until fall.

The warbler cousins came to Loon in a large flock just as the birch and aspen were turning yellow and sprinkling golden coins on the cool water of the streams and lakes.

"We want to leave now," they told Loon. "It's getting hard to find food now and the chilly nights are becoming uncomfortable and long."

"I can't start the trip yet," said Loon. "I agreed to wait as late in the fall as possible. Try to wait longer."

As the maples flamed with autumn colors and ice ringed still pools on frosty mornings, the dabbling ducks came to Loon. "We want to go now," they said with loud, impatient quacks. "It's cold in the morning and the shallows where we like to dabble is beginning to freeze. Soon there will be no food for us."

"We agreed to wait," said Loon. "I can't begin the trip south just yet. Try to wait longer."

Finally, when all the trees shed their leaves in great swirls of color on stormy winds and the ice around the edges of the lakes was thickening and reaching toward deep water and the first winter snows were stinging eyes with cold, the great flocks of Canada Geese came to Loon to ask that the trip south begin. Their honking and squawking was deafening. Owl, himself, came to Loon. "Oh, please," he said, "take them away from here! Go south now! Leave us in peace for the winter!"

Loon smiled and agreed. He raced across the lake until his beating wings found enough air beneath them to lift his heavy body onto the wind. Eagerly the warblers and ducks and geese took to their wings in flocks so thick they darkened

the skies like autumn storms.

But Loon, who had only taken leadership to end the bickering, was not a very good navigator. At the head of the great dark clouds of birds, he had trouble finding the right way. If it had not been for Snipe who flew at his shoulder the whole way, none of the birds would ever have found the way to their winter resting spots. The flocks realized just how poor Loon was at finding his way and complained in angry voices.

"I agree," said Loon. "I am not the leader you need. In fact, I think Snipe would be your best choice. He travels farther than most who go south and we can join up with him when he comes again north."

"But Owl and Jay won't let me be leader in the summer," said Snipe.

"Owl and Jay and Crow do not travel south." said Loon. "We don't have to tell them our agreement. In the summer I am content to be leader. In the winter, Owl is leader for northern birds and Snipe can lead our trip south."

It was agreed. All the birds were finally happy, even Jay who found a profit in waiting on Owl's table. As for Loon, he never did find out how to get south in the fall. He can often be seen at the end of a long skein of geese to keep from losing his way.

The little boy grinned with pride and pleasure when he finished his tale and handed the drum to the old man. His grandfather took it and chuckled. "You two boys seem to have napped through my storytelling as the baby is doing now. Somehow you have mixed the legends I told you with dreams from the fertile imaginations of your youth. But then, if stories were never changed from time to time, people would become bored with their telling and the tales would be lost. I would hope, however, that at least some of the time you two share legends, you choose the sure flight of the snipe and not the wandering course of the loon."

Several around the fire chuckled and the boys looked down. But the grandfather was not really admonishing them. He leaned over and hugged the smaller lad while he patted the knee of the older one.

"Never mind our amusement," he whispered. "The best tales of all are the ones we remember because they are humorous and clever."

Mary Jo Pauly

How Language Was Lost

fter the drum had been passed back to the old man and the boys were joking again back and forth about whose legend was the best, the handsome young man reached toward the old man.

"I have a story I would like to tell," he said, "and right now might be the perfect time for it."

"Oh?" said the old man as he handed over the drum. "What tale do you have in mind?"

The man smiled and looked from the teasing boys to the woman with the baby and then back to the old man. "The story of how language was lost."

"Oh, yes!" agreed the old man. "I had forgotten that one. Yes, I do believe this is just the time for it to be told. Listen, boys. Listen to this story."

A loon's voice rose from the darkened lake. As was usual, the people around the fire hushed to listen and did not speak again until the loon's song was over.

"Do you know what the loon says?" asked the younger of the brothers. There was a snicker in his tone.

"No," said the man seriously and somewhat sadly. "But

there was a time a long, long while ago when people who sat around their campfire would have known what the loon was saying."

"How could that be?" challenged the little boy. "How could people long ago know what the loon was saying and we don't know any of it at all?"

"We lost the common language."

"Common language? What common language?"

"Hush," said the man, exasperation seeping into his tone. "Hush, and I will tell you the story of how the language was lost."

There was a time when there was only one language. It was a time almost before time, when the world was new and the creatures still seeking their paths and roles. The waters were sweet and the skies clear of storms. It was a time when Creator still walked along the paths and spoke freely with his creatures, a time of peace and magic.

The people and the beasts had but one language so they could speak to each other. This was a time, of course, before people became hunters. How could they hunt creatures who could explain to them why they wished to live? Neither did the wolf pursue the deer for the deer would plead for its life, nor the owl kill the rabbit who could beg mercy. But the peace of that magical time did not last very long.

The Creator had given each of his creatures ways to be happy. He had taught the birds to fly and the fish to swim. The wolf could run on swift, tireless legs and the lynx pad on soundless paws. To man, he had given many things. He had given him the ability to walk and carry at the same time. He had made people fast runners, good swimmers and knowledgeable of the resources of the lake country and forest. Hands could make tools, shelters, musical instruments. The greatest gift Creator gave his creatures was the ability to know when they were happy, to feel joy.

But though the ability to feel joy was a great, powerful gift, it also had its dangers. If a being could know when he was truly happy, he could also know when he was not. Great joy is like a flower whose bloom is spectacular but brief. And when the blossom fades—always too quickly—other joys had to be sought. There is also the problem that a joy for one is not necessarily a joy for another. Because Creator tried very hard to make his creatures different so that each

could benefit differently from the world, he had also created
in them different views of joy. One could find pleasure in
the soft light of a forest thicket; another found sadness there
and looked to open meadows and the sun.

But Creator had not known that his creatures would
find the desire for joy so overpowering that each sought
only his own happiness and did not consider the tastes and
needs of others. Soon Creator found that the people and
animals were bickering with each other, selfishly pushing
aside the small creatures like the mouse and the rabbit. The
wolf pursued the deer if the deer got in his way for he so loved
to run and chase. The bear lumbered over the homes of mice
with no concern. Man made his villages and chopped down
trees for firewood even if the clearings belonged to other
beasts and the trees were home to many families of birds.
Even amongst their own kind, the beasts and people squabbled
and argued.

Creator was distressed. His beautiful world was no longer
the pleasant place of song and merriment. Instead of singing
wonderful melodies, birds squawked irritably. The lynx
hissed and spat and the bear popped his great teeth. The
wonderful common language Creator had given to all the
creatures alike was not being used when so many creatures
found others so irritating. And because humans were the
most gifted of the creatures in many ways, the most powerful because of their minds, they were becoming the most
difficult creatures with whom to get along.

Then there came a time when people no longer used
their hands to build shelters and instruments to create music.
Weapons were made instead. These were used to drive off
other creatures—even other people—who got in the way of
the pursuit of joy. Creator's peaceful world of music and

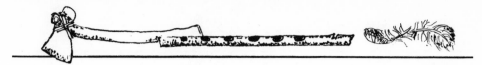

happiness became an ugly battlefield where people and beasts were being injured and killed. It had to stop.

And so Creator called all his creatures together. He laid out a great feast before them and told them to eat and be happy. As arguments broke out over who should sit at the Creator's hand, who should receive which platter of food and who should be served first, Creator drew away from them. He stepped into his canoe and paddled just off shore. From there he called to his creatures.

"Quiet!" he shouted to them in a tone he had never used before. It was a sound like thunder and fierce wind.

The people and animals were instantly stilled.

"I do not want to hear you abuse the beautiful voices I gave you," he told them. "I gave you voice so you could share the wonder and beauty of the world around you with one another. Each of you has a different view. Language was made to share that difference. But you have not done this."

All were quiet, listening to Creator and becoming afraid.

"I have given each of you so much," Creator told them, "yet you do not see what I gave you. You see what the next one has and want it too. You do not share. You do not love. You do not even leave each other in peace! Not one of you is blameless; not one of you is without shame. How can I stay among you when you fight and argue and kill each other?"

The people and animals began to mutter to each other, not really understanding what Creator was telling them.

As Creator's canoe drifted slowly further from the land, everyone crowded the pebbly shore. Some, like the loon and the duck waded into the shallows but were too afraid of Creator's unusual anger to paddle after him.

Creator's voice was filled with sorrow when he said, "I gave you voices to make song. You shout and curse. I gave

you instruments to make music. You turn them into weapons
to hurt and kill. I gave you a common language so that you
could communicate between yourselves and share the per-
spective of your unique lives. This gift seems to be of no use
to you at all. And yet this of all the gifts I gave to you is the
greatest and most wonderful. This, then, is what I take from
you. Go. Go live your lives and make of them what you can.
You will discover that the world will not be so pleasant a
place without my presence. Find happiness if you can. Perhaps the process of living will convince you that joy is a luxury
to be treasured and shared, not a life in itself."

Creator's canoe was now quite a distance from shore.
The loon, suddenly realizing that he was leaving them forever,
swam out toward it. In the common language the loon begged
Creator to give them another chance and stay among them.
Creator shook his head.

"I cannot stay," Creator said sadly. "Not now . . . not until
there is an end to the fighting. But I will tell you this, Loon.
Call me back when my joyful place is restored. If this can
happen, I will return."

Then the canoe sped away at a remarkable speed, quickly
receding into the distant horizon.

The people and animals just stared after the canoe. It was
almost as if they were entranced. Only when Creator was gone
did they look about themselves and move back from the
shore. It was then that the meaning of Creator's words began
to be impressed upon them.

A duck quacked and seemed genuinely startled by its
voice. It began to quack rapidly and flap about the shore in
dismay. A raven croaked hoarsely, then startled and flew off
to the tops of the pines. A lynx yowled, then hissed. The wolves
growled amongst themselves and crawled off into the forest.

The owl hooted, and a mouse squeaked in terror and ran away.

All the animals were scattering, seeking sheltered places where they could learn to understand what had happened to them. Soon only the small group of people were left on the shore. They looked at each other with wide eyes, afraid to open their mouths for fear of the awful sound that would emerge. Finally, a young man tried his voice. It was a noise not unlike the quack of the duck in a way; his complaint was the whine of the lynx. Another spoke—a growl like the wolf's. Another had a croak like the raven.

The people covered their mouths, then their faces and wept. A baby wailed and its mother was so dismayed at the sound that she handed it to a sister and fled into the shadows of the forest.

From off shore the loon had watched them all. He had heard the many new and unfamiliar voices of the people and the animals. He was afraid to try his own voice for fear it would be as awful as the rest. Perhaps he would have the quack of the duck . . . or worse. Still, silence was an unpleasant sound also. Loon inhaled deeply and then filled his breath with song. Wonderfully, magically, his voice was unchanged! Loon of all the creatures had retained the language originally given by the Creator.

And so, loon sings as Creator had taught. But his song is mostly sad and lonesome for loon knows that the world will never return to the primal peace Creator first made. That time is past.

The younger boy flapped his arms and quacked like a duck. The older brother was about to elbow him but stopped and turned to the man.

"I don't think people sound like ducks now," he said, "and my mother can sing as pretty as a warbler. Did people voices change?"

The man shook his head. "Not really. But one of the gifts Creator had originally given man was the ability to mimic the voices of animals around him. I guess over time, man found a voice—a new voice, mind you—that was not so ugly as the one that night after Creator left. Or maybe ... or maybe we just got used to the racket that comes out of our mouths."

The young man fell silent, thinking, then abruptly handed the drum back to the old man. The old man took it and held it up to the light of the fire.

"You know," the old man finally said, "Creator gave us a gift that night when he left. He gave us the ability to wonder. How dull our world would be if there were no mystery in it, nor the ability to wonder so that we could appreciate it."

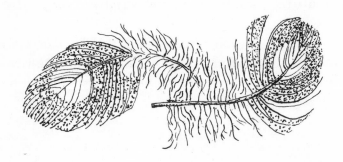

Cindy Pintok

Mary Jo Pauly

The Loon and the Wolf

The shy young woman spoke. "But it didn't stay that way, did it? Some creatures speak to each other, don't they?"

The young man looked around the jealous sister who tried to keep her face between the handsome man's and that of her shy sister.

"Well, of course it did," the man said softly, confused. "Can you talk to the beasts? There is no language between us and them nor between one beast and another."

Just then, from the blackness of the night, a wolf howled. Its note was far off, sad and deep. Almost as if in response, the loon out on the lake sent the rising note of its wail after the wolf's howl. The two notes were not the same; the wolf had a lower voice with more resonance and power than did the loon. But the two songs fit together in harmony, in mood, and in pattern. They both rose high in the night stillness and held the final note like the pines held wind.

The wolf howled again. The loon answered. The shy woman smiled, her face easily prettier than her sister's scowl.

"There, you see!" she exclaimed, her voice musical and soft. "They seem to have the same language when they sing...

different, but still the same. And they *do* sing together."

"I seem to remember there is a legend about this," said the young man. "Do you know this story?"

The shy woman's smile fell and she looked down into the folds of fabric on her lap. She did not look up, was not brave enough to meet his eyes, but she nodded.

Though the woman did not see it, the young man smiled. The woman with the baby saw the smile, however, and showed her approval with a slight tip of her head and a sparkle in her eyes. The young man's blush in response was lost in the fire's glow. Without a word, the man took the drum being offered by the old man. He reached past the jealous sister and set the drum by the bowed woman's knee.

The sister, older by several years and enamoured of the handsome man, tried to snatch the drum away from her sister's knee. But the man had seemed to know this might happen and was ready. He gripped her wrist firmly and slowly placed the woman's hand back in her own lap.

The sister was angered by this, but chose not to interfere again. She folded her arms over her chest and looked away, out into the darkness of the lake.

The shy young woman looked up just briefly, just enough to offer a soft smile of gratitude to the man. He did not frighten her by smiling back. She looked down at the drum at her knee and slowly reached toward it, took it and drew it into her lap. Then she waited while she settled her soul.

Instead of tapping at the drum, she slowly began to run two graceful fingers around the taut skin of the top, just inside the rim. This created a quiet circle of sound, like the flutter of a grouse's wings at a distance. Only when the pattern took hold of her mind could she draw in the courage to tell her tale.

Stonefeather was an old loon who lived alone on a small bay of a large lake. It was a time of lengthening summer warmth when the green of the lake country had reached full growth but had not yet receded to browns and yellows. Insects hummed their incessant drones, and throngs of black-comma tadpoles darkened the shallows where the ducks dabbled and the moose waded to chew the water lilies, the mud sucking at their big hooves and water streaming down their dewlaps. A lynx and her kittens hunted just at the edge of the raspberry thickets.

The old loon kept to the deep water and hunted the fish that flashed through the cold depths. His life was quiet, and his days were spent alone. In the evening, Stonefeather would listen to the symphony of loon voices. The huge lake, with its many bays and islands and connecting waterways, was a system of water during the day; at night it was a system of song. But Stonefeather was not a part of the community of song. He had not found a mate that year, nor the year before. In the law of the loons, an unmated loon was not allowed to sing after the spring mating time. Some nights Stonefeather ached to join the other loons, but he was forbidden to do so.

In that same country were several packs of wolves that hunted the dark forest like the loons hunted the dark water. At night they also sang. But when the loons sang, the wolves were silent; and if the wolves began first, the loons swam out to the deepest waters and listened, but did not intrude upon the wolves' night with their melody.

It happened that one old wolf had been driven out of its pack because he could no longer hunt. Since it was summer and there were plenty of mice and voles in the grasses around the bay, the old wolf had been able to live on his own even

though he was very lame and his teeth were worn nearly to the gum. He took up residence on a little hump of land which sat between Stonefeather's bay and the main lake. It was almost a rock island except that a swampy strip of land connected it to the forest on one side. The other side had been joined to the island at one time by a beaver's dam. But the lodge had been destroyed and the beavers were gone. The dam was breached along most of its length, giving Stonefeather access to the main lake.

The wolf found a cavity that the crooked pines' roots had split in the rock, and made the hump of land his home. At night the wolf climbed to the top of the rocks and listened to the wolves or the loons chorus through the darkness. He too was forbidden to sing for he was exiled.

But a wolf is an even more social creature than the loon; the old wolf finally could not contain the music within him. One night loneliness drove the old wolf to lift his silvered muzzel in song before any of the other wolves or the loons had begun to sing.

The note began very low and slow. It rose along minor chords and arched above the deepening dusk. The wolf sang out his loneliness, his sorrow at being apart from the pack which he had led for ten years, and his frustration at being lame and old. Several times the wolf carried his note to the stars. Then he fell silent. In the quiet that followed, no wolf or loon sang. Even as the night spread from the shadows of the forest and rose from the depths of the lake, the only voices were from the multitude of small creatures—the crickets and mosquitoes—and the constant lap of the water against the many shores.

The next night, the old wolf sang again from his hump of land. The song was the same, a song of sorrow and loneli-

ness. Following the solo, as before, no voices challenged the stillness of the night.

On the third night, the loons began early and blended their voices with the rich colors of the sunset. But at the height of their song, when the fabric of the melody was a tapestry of many voices, the low note of the old wolf cut through the loon's voices like a knife. When the wolf's song was ended, no loon sang. The night again filled up with silence as it filled up with the hidden colors of night.

The next night, the wolves tried to take their turn at singing, but before their symphony was well begun, the lone wolf interrupted with his deep, sad note. This time, as the night threatened to swallow all sound, Stonefeather broke the long silence he had steadfastly maintained. He sailed his note after the wolf's, and by doing so, exiled himself from the loon community forever. So was their law.

After Stonefeather sang, there was a softer quiet. Then the wolf sang again. Soon the night was filled with the melody of the duet. Long into the darkness, long after the loons of the lake were asleep on the waves and the wolves of the forest off on the hunt, the two old singers wove their voices together. And as the stars wheeled over the moon-sparkled lake country, the tone of the voices changed. The sadness of the wolf's song became a ringing joy. The loon's voice, long unused, at first lacked depth and range; but as that evening and the next days and weeks passed, it took on all the beauty it had had when the loon had been young. Within the resonance of each other's song, the two solitary old creatures found that precious companionship that each had lost.

As the summer ripened into fall and the maples flamed and the grasses at the shore of the lake lost their color, becoming as crisp as fallen leaves, the old wolf and the loon

77

continued to sing each night. Skeins of geese, their voices filled with the urgency of cold, raced against torn clouds and darkened winds. Still the pair sang. The adult loons followed the geese on migration and then the dusky young took to uncertain wings. The wolf packs, dissolved to families in the summer months, began to draw together and move from the den sites deeper into the forest. But even when the crisp mornings rimmed the still bay with ice, the old loon could not leave the lake country for he knew he would never return, and the wolf was reluctant to depart from the windy rock of his home for he knew the winter would take his life.

Storm after storm blew into the mouth of the little bay, slamming hard against the hump of rock and twisting the new growth of the crooked pines. But except for those nights when the harsh music of the wind and rain overpowered their voices, the wolf and the loon continued to sing. But now in their song was a certainty that their special bond would not last, could not last.

Snow flew on high winds. The ice that gathered among the reeds and along the shore no longer melted in the thinning heat of the afternoon. The skin began to stretch out over the water. And then, one bitter morning after a still, cold night, Stonefeather woke to see that the mouth of the bay was iced shut. Now, unless he crossed the ice to the main lake, he could never again take wing for there was not length enough in the narrow bay for him to race over the water and take wing.

That night the loon sang again, this time the tone of his song was joy not sorrow. Stonefeather had decided to sing as wonderfully as he could until he could sing no more. The wolf answered in kind. For him, too, the winter was certain death without the support of his pack.

The bay froze that night. All the next day Stonefeather

crouched in the cold wind and moved laboriously over the ice by gathering his feet under him as best he could, then humping forward. Many times his webbed feet just slipped and his broad keel never lifted off the ice, but the sight of the blue water just beyond the beaver dam enticed him on. By evening he had made it as far as the first dam log. The water ahead, deep blue and ruffled by wind, was very close. It was then the lynx spotted him

The long, whiskered ears of the bigger of the two lynx kittens popped up from behind the ruined beaver lodge when Stonefeathers toes scraped the ice and his keel *plopped* ahead another few inches. The kitten peeked at him, then sank out of sight—all except the tips of his ears. But Stonefeather had seen him and knew how dangerous his situation was. He scrambled with his toes again and pushed himself another inch forward. He tried to watch and not to watch the tassled ears.

Another set of tufted ears flicked up from the logs of the lodge—the second kitten. With a bound, the bigger male cleared the hole in the top of the beaver's old lodge. The smaller female followed. Both lynx kittens scrambled over tangled branches and icy logs. In just a moment they were circling Stonefeather, batting at him with oversized mitts of paws.

Stonefeather hissed and croaked hoarsely at them. He stabbed at the thrusted paws with his sharp bill, connecting with the smaller kitten's pad. The little lynx yowled and spit angrily, but drew back. This caused the brother to be more cautious and circle warily.

Stonefeather tried to keep an eye on each of them, but when the male lynx was on the opposite side of him from the little female, she leaped at him and took the tip of one wing

in her teeth.

Stonefeather snapped his head around to jab at her, but the male lynx pounced on his other wing. Now Stonefeather was stretched between them and could reach neither. And though the kittens together could not lift him, they managed to drag the loon quite effectively some ten feet closer to the shore. Then Stonefeather saw the mother lynx at the edge of the woods, watching.

The mother lynx was just making her way toward Stonefeather and the kittens, picking her way over the iced lodge carefully, when she stopped and arched her back, increasing in size dramatically. Stonefeather, his eyes fixed on her, almost failed to realize that the kittens had dropped his wings and were scampering quickly toward their mother, looking back in quick, frightened glances.

Stonefeather turned to look behind him. He was face to face with a head nearly the length of his body and wide, oblique, yellow eyes. A great mouth opened and closed over his shoulders.

Stonefeather was too stunned to strike out, too stunned at first to realize that the jaws that could crack the leg bone of a moose had not penetrated his insulating layer of feathers. He was half lifted, half dragged to the hump of land next to the beaver dam and carried up the rocks to a depression between the lichen-covered rocks and roots of the pines. He was plopped down in the thick duff of pine needles and rolled onto his keel. He looked up just as the wolf limped away around the rocks.

For many minutes Stonefather stared at the crisp line of grey-green rock against clear blue sky. Slowly fear slipped away and the puffs of air clouding from his open bill became little wisps of fog from his nostrils. The sun eased below the

crystal horizon of the lake. Stars like sun-sparkled snow filled the sky.

Stonefeather knew by the feel of the wind and the deepening of the cold that the main lake would be frozen by morning. Without open water he could not live. But instead of settling into death, the old loon lifted his bill in song.

Stonefeather sang as he had done so many nights out on the bay. His wail was long, well-modulated and smooth. And when he stopped to catch his breath, the wolf answered him. The great, gaunt beast sat just feet away, his sparse ruff outlined by the circle of the rising moon. Clouds of mist rose up from his jaws which were tilted to the stars.

The wolf heaved himself up and painfully limped to where the loon lay. He sat, his bony hip too naked of flesh to warm Stonefeather's side. But he sang, and the rumble of his deep notes crossed into Stonefeather's body even as the treble of the old loon's chords passed to the wolf.

They sang deep into the night. At dawn, the cold on the wind was crackling through the stiff needles of the pines. It ruffled the fur of the wolf's back as he lay curled about the still body of the old loon. Stonefeather's head rested on the wolf's paws. The wolf's great head lay across Stonefeather's neck.

The pair were said to have been found that way. It is also said that the magic they made that last night as they sang curled together made it possible for the wolves and loons of all generations afterwards to sing together, to bridge the gap in their languages by song.

It was very quiet around the fire when this tale was finished. The two boys had finally succumbed to sleep, one against the old man who also nodded and the other curled on the ground. The jealous sister had retired from the fireside and the mother with the baby had eased back into shadows.

The shy woman was embarrassed by the quiet and lowered her head as she handed the drum back to the handsome man to give to the old man. He reached for the drum with both hands, one took the drum and set it softly at the old man's knee, the other took the young woman's hand. She met his eyes and smiled.

From the shadows beyond the circle of firelight, the woman with the child hummed a quiet approval.

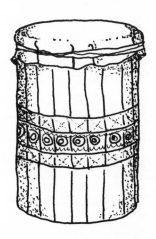

Mark Coyle

Mark Coyle

Epilogue

The fire burned low. The flames that had whirled in wild, pagan dance, now flickered softly, red coals coated in ash. The great feast of wood was gone. Silence had replaced the crackle and roaring; lake mist cooled the heat of the fire's glow. One by one the coals winked out like stars sheathed in clouds.

The people who had told the tales and kept the rhythm of the fire in the circle drawn tight like the skin of the drum were gone now. The drum lay forgotten and still.

The wind soughed through the pines and stirred the lake's skin to wrinkles that lapped the shore. A cricket's tired chirp punctuated the shadows that drifted endlessly into night.

There is the illusion that night is the same as day, minus the sun; or worse, that night is the absence of day. Night is its own separate universe, one vastly different from the universe of day. And although all earth's creatures exist through both realms, few creatures have their essence tied to both.

During the daylight hours the great horned owl is an over-stuffed caricature on a branch, pestered with impunity by songbirds and the butt of the jays' cacophonous humor.

But after the songbirds and jays have fled to their roosts at the passing of the sun, the owl bestirs itself and draws in the essence of night. To the small furred creatures of that universe, the owl is a whisper of wings and a whorl of crushing, ebony talons. At night the owl is death. The jay, by day the clever entrepreneur and tormentor of the out-of-world owl, by night is virtually non-existent.

So it is with all creatures—bold in one realm, meek in the other; a danger in one, a joke in the other. Further, the character of the land and water—the very air—changes with day and night. During the day the sky is finite, a closed-over blue dome with the sun as chandelier. At night the sky opens up on the universe, revealing the earth as a speck in the multitude of the racing heavens. The jay would be awed if he knew.

Twilight is the special time, often accompanied by colors and odors not truly a part of either great realm. It is a dangerous time when the creatures of both realms are slightly out of place. It is a haunting, magical time—a time of legends—and sometimes seemingly devoid of players . . . save the loon.

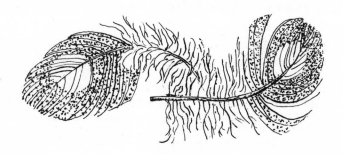

The Author

Loon Legends is Corinne Dwyer's second book, her first fiction. A graduate of the College of St. Benedict, St. Joseph, Minnesota, with a B.A. in Biology, she has maintained a strong interest in nature coupled with writing. Corinne works as a book designer for a small press and is the editor for the Stearns County Historical Society (central Minnesota). She lives on a small farm with her husband John and three daughters— Cecelia, Miranda and Elizabeth Ann. The farm grows cockleburs, Shetland ponies and Airedale terriers. Corinne is a member of the Central Minnesota Writers' Workshop.

The Illustrator

Mark was abandoned as a child by his parents in the late Cretaceous Period (80 million years ago). In a land and time devoid of human life, teeming with Tyrannosaurus Rex and Triceratops, life was a struggle for survival. Fighting his way up through the ages, Mark learned basic drawing from the cave people in Lascaux, France. Eons later he studied with Raphael, then Watteau and eventually with the French Impressionists, Degas and Monet among them. Mr. Coyle is currently residing in the late 20th century.